Roll Cyrus Roll

The Adventures of Cyrus the Colt

This is the story of a unique colt named Cyrus who dreams of becoming a famous racehorse.

Cyrus gets excited for bath time. He splashes in the spray from the hose and enjoys the cool water running down his back. Cyrus has fuzzy ears, and when he shakes his head at bath time, the farmer gets soaked by the spray.

Getting washed is part of everyone's routine, but there is still something that makes Cyrus different.

After getting clean, all the horses go to the sand pit.
They all gather around the warm, white sand and then
lie down on their sides. They kick their feet up into the air
and roll back and forth creating a cloud.
Rolling in the sand is a messy way to scratch your back.
It also makes the farmer growl after he just gave them all baths!
Rolling in the sand is what Cyrus won't do.
The other horses wondered why Cyrus would not roll.

Cyrus' mom also loves to roll in the sand and pressures him to roll too.
"All horses roll," she proclaims.

She worries that Cyrus doesn't know how to roll.

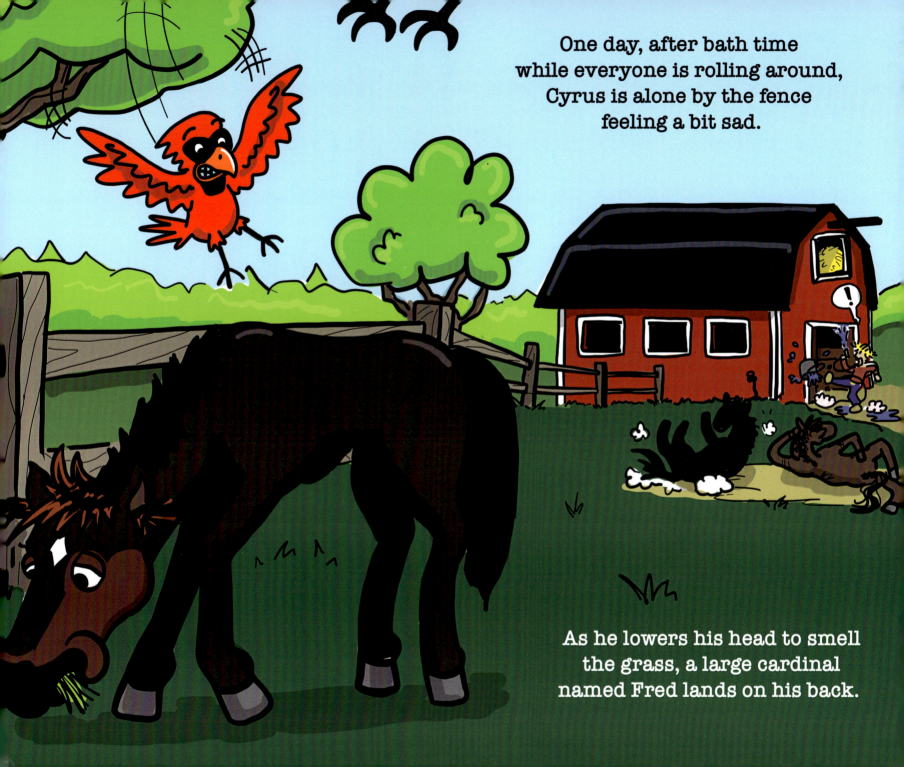

One day, after bath time while everyone is rolling around, Cyrus is alone by the fence feeling a bit sad.

As he lowers his head to smell the grass, a large cardinal named Fred lands on his back.

Fred's claws scratch Cyrus' itchy back. They also tickle a little!
"I see you don't like rolling, so I figured this was a safe place
to be," proclaims Fred.

"I was getting chased by a mean old crow.
Do you mind if I hang out with you for a little?"
the bird asks.

Cyrus enjoys having someone scratch his back and
talk to him while everyone else rolls in the sand.

The new friends roam the fields together every day.
Cyrus cherishes having someone who does not mind if he is different.
Fred tells Cyrus jokes like
"Why do you wear horseshoes but not horse socks?"
and
"When you are sick, do you go to the horsepital?"

Finally it is time to go to Racing School, and Cyrus is the best in his class! The trainers at Racing School have never seen a colt so skilled, shiny and clean.

To Mom and Dad. - B.F.

"Roll Cyrus Roll
The Adventures of Cyrus the Colt"
Written by Designated Hitters Racing, LLC
Story by Chris Brown
Illustrated by Ben Fidler

Published by
Designated Hitters Racing, LLC
ISBN: 978-0-578-85499-1
Copyright © 2021 Designated Hitters Racing, LLC

For more information on the Thoroughbred Retirement Foundation
Go to: www.trfinc.org

All rights reserved. No part of this book may be reproduced
in any form on or by an electronic or mechanical means, including
information storage and retrieval systems, without permission
in writing from the publisher, except by a reviewer who may quote
brief passages in a review.

Second Printing April 2021

Printed in the USA by Lightning Press, Totowa, NJ